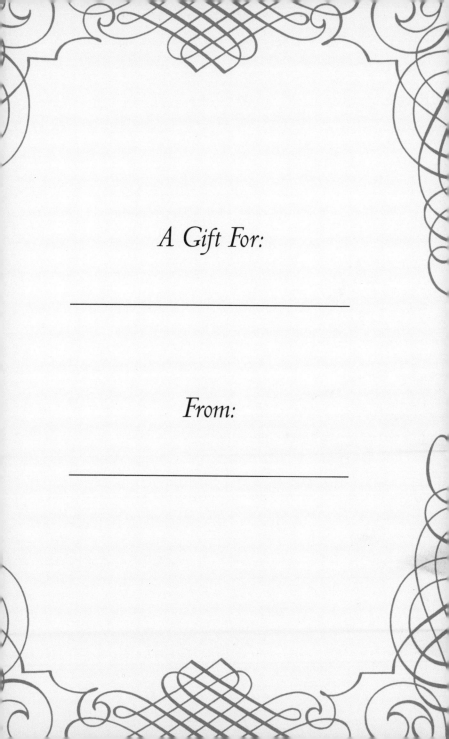

A Gift For:

_____

From:

_____

Copyright © 2012 Hallmark Licensing, LLC
Text copyright © 2012 by Lance Wubbels

Published by Hallmark Gift Books,
a division of Hallmark Cards, Inc.,
Kansas City, MO 64141
Visit us on the Web at Hallmark.com.

All rights reserved. No part of this publication
may be reproduced, transmitted, or stored
in any form or by any means without the prior
written permission of the publisher.

Scripture taken from the Holy Bible: New International Version®. NIV®.
Copyright © 1973, 1978, 1984 by International Bible Society.
Used by permission of Zondervan.

Editorial Director: Delia Berrigan
Editor: Jared Smith
Art Director: Chris Opheim
Designer: Rob Latimer
Production Designer: Dan Horton

ISBN: 978-1-59530-534-3
BOK1203

Printed and bound in China
SEP12

THE LORD IS MY SHEPHERD

Inspiration
from the
Book of
Psalms

LANCE WUBBELS

Hallmark
gift books

INTRODUCTION

The Book of Psalms is the most widely read, best-known, and most loved book in the Bible. For three thousand years its soothing words have calmed anxious hearts, rekindled courage in the fearful, and comforted the grieving. Because it addresses the soul in all its aspirations, desires, sorrows, and trials, and offers a message of light and hope to its readers, it is a resource countless people consult every day for inspiration, consolation, and inner strength.

Many of the psalms are poems set to music and were sung during temple worship or on other appointed Jewish religious days. The word for psalms in the Hebrew Bible is *Tehillim*, which means "praise." Our English word psalms comes from the Greek word *psalmoi*, which originally meant "a song or a poem sung with instrumental accompaniment."

As such, the Book of Psalms is the world's oldest hymnal in continuous use and contains some of the most moving and profound expressions of the human heart ever written. A number of the psalms remember and celebrate the significant events of the history of the Hebrew people. Most of the psalms, however, are prayers—not merely forms of devotion, but the heartfelt utterances of writers desperate for God. All of their experiences—whether they involve acute suffering or indescribable joy—are viewed in direct relation to God.

THE PSALMS EXPRESS EVERY HUMAN EMOTION

One reason the Book of Psalms remains so important is because it expresses all the emotions of the human experience in reflective detail: love, joy, hope, sadness, doubt, fear, despair, distress, grief, depression, anger, revenge, anxiety, desperation, humility, and victory. Wherever you are in your life journey, you will find a place in the psalms that resonates with your heart.

It is remarkable to think that thousands of years ago our deepest experiences were written for us! It is as though the psalmists knew our souls through and through and expressed all that we think and feel. The psalms cut across age differences, transcend cultural barriers, and have their own universal language. The hearts of people across the world have felt the same pains, carried the same burdens, wept the same tears, and cried out for the same answers!

One Constant Thread of Worship

One emotional and spiritual thread is seamlessly woven into the fabric of the entire Book of Psalms: worship to almighty God. As God's children, we were created to praise and worship Him, and expressions of praise and thanksgiving are found in almost every psalm. From contemplative worship, to exuberant praise, to the deepest prayer of the heart, the psalms demonstrate the center of true worship and faith at all times—even in the trying times. Some of the psalms are intensely personal, others are defiant, and still others are filled with awe. But whether they were written in a temple or a cave, all have one purpose: to help us in our worship. The variety of the types of psalms demonstrates that we all worship differently, and God welcomes us just as we are.

The psalmists were often not content to merely lift up their voices in worship. To these they added the accompaniment of harps and cymbals, organs and trumpets. Indeed, more than one of the psalmists called upon all of nature to aid in their worship. Whatsoever had a voice or could make a sound was to give God praise. Every flower and every star, every stream and every hill, joined to swell the anthem of His praise.

The Psalmists

King David (1000 BC) is often accredited with writing the Book of Psalms and is referred to as "the sweet psalmist of Israel" or "the hero of Israel's songs" (2 Samuel 23:1). By far, David's psalms dominate this book, and for good reason. Perhaps more than any other Bible character, David exemplifies the most essential elements of worship: humility, repentance, and a deep desire for intimacy with God.

But David is not the only author of the psalms. The writing of the Book of Psalms spans about a thousand years, from the time of Moses (about 1500 BC) through the lives of Solomon, Asaph, Heman, and the sons of Korah, who were the appointed temple singers, to the time of Ezra (about 450 BC). Many of the psalms were written anonymously.

The Bible within the Bible

The Book of Psalms is found in the middle of the Bible and is sometimes called "the Bible within the Bible" because it summarizes what precedes and anticipates what follows. All the other parts of the Bible are touched upon in the psalms. There creation is repeated; there the deliverance of the Jewish nation from Egypt, the giving of the Law at Mount Sinai, and the long years in the wilderness are remembered; there the captivity and the return of the Jewish people from captivity are set forth; there the birth of Christ is anticipated and His suffering and death on the Cross is expressed in remarkable detail; and there the coming of the Church is sketched.

The Book of Psalms is actually divided into five hymn books, which is thought by many to correlate to the Torah, the first five books of the Bible:

Book I (Psalms 1–41)
Book II (Psalms 42–72)
Book III (Psalms 73–89)
Book IV (Psalms 90–106)
Book V (Psalms 107–150)

THE PSALMS AND YOU

Many readers find the psalms to be their dearest companion in dark hours of loneliness and discouragement, and their greatest encourager in times of celebration and adoration. Hidden within, they find "the music of the heart"! As you read, make these psalms your own. Don't just read them silently—pray them, sing them, experience them, and embrace their honesty. Let them lead you in worship. As you do, you will find power and comfort in the knowledge that "The LORD is my shepherd, I lack nothing" (Psalm 23:1) and "Your word is a lamp for my feet, a light on my path" (Psalm 119:105).

PSALM 1

Blessed is the one
    who does not walk in step with the wicked
or stand in the way that sinners take
    or sit in the company of mockers,
but whose delight is in the law of the Lord,
    and who meditates on his law day and night.
That person is like a tree planted by streams of water,
    which yields its fruit in season
and whose leaf does not wither—
    whatever they do prospers.

Not so the wicked!
    They are like chaff that the wind blows away.
Therefore the wicked will not stand in the judgment,
    nor sinners in the assembly of the righteous.

For the Lord watches over the way of the righteous,
    but the way of the wicked leads to destruction.

Here, the psalmist describes a lovely image of a vast and majestic tree, grand and dignified and beautiful—a vision that lingers with us long after we have gazed upon it. Its branches stretch out over gentle, flowing streams of water, bringing abundant fruit in season as well as refreshment for those seeking comforts beneath its shadows. The tree's great roots grip the ground and have sunk deep into the oozy riverbanks, tapping into an inexhaustible supply.

In a land where flowing spring-fed streams are scarce, this tree has been deliberately planted near streams of water so that even if one stream should fail, it has others from which to draw. When the hot winds blow and drought is upon the land, the trees not planted near the streams wither and die; but this tree's leaves remain all year round like an evergreen.

Such is the characterization of the person "whose delight is in the law of the LORD [Jehovah], and who meditates on his law day and night." He has made the streams of God's grace his never-failing source of life and sustenance. He does not depend on the ever-changing world around him. The secret of his flourishing strength and beauty is found by living a life saturated with the Word of God.

We all have resources upon which we draw. The paramount question is, Where are our roots? Our lives should be rooted deeply in the spiritual resources of God's grace, for where God is, there will never be a lack of supply. A life separated from God, on the other hand, cannot grow, cannot be at rest; it will be the victim of circumstance, frightened by surprises and alarmed by countless fears. We must stop looking to other people to give our lives meaning and happiness, and give God's truth the time to permeate our souls. We must be still and know that He is God.

And so this tree "yields its fruit in season." If our roots are deep in the Word of God, we will have the love, the forgiving spirit, the strength and courage, the patience and perseverance that the Word of God produces in believers' lives. We will not only be fruitful people, but even our leaves, our little deeds of love and our quiet words of encouragement, will not wither away and be forgotten.

Finally, "whatever they do prospers." Now, this is a truly happy person. But the fulfillment of this promise cannot be measured by our outward prosperity. Instead, we prosper in the sense that no matter what happens, we find strength for the day and hope in the midst of the hardest difficulties. This requires the eye of faith to see, and by this faith we perceive our soul's true prosperity, even if everything seems to go against us.

PSALM 8

Lord, our Lord,
  how majestic is your name in all the earth!

You have set your glory
  in the heavens.
Through the praise of children and infants
  you have established a stronghold against your enemies,
  to silence the foe and the avenger.
When I consider your heavens,
  the work of your fingers,
the moon and the stars,
  which you have set in place,
what is mankind that you are mindful of them,
  human beings that you care for them?

You have made them a little lower than the angels
  and crowned them with glory and honor.
You made them rulers over the works of your hands;
  you put everything under their feet:
all flocks and herds,
  and the animals of the wild,
the birds in the sky,
  and the fish in the sea,
  all that swim the paths of the seas.

Lord, our Lord,
  how majestic is your name in all the earth!

To capture the essence of this psalm, we should read or sing it beneath the starry heavens in a wilderness place, for David presumably was inspired to write it while in just such a location. He gazed up at the seemingly infinite expanse that spread above and around him, and then in his imagination he lifted off from earth, soared into the stratosphere of space, and wandered among the billions of stars in our galaxy and billions of distant galaxies in the universe. Rather than envisioning a dark and lifeless cosmos, he saw a universe teeming with the splendor of God's presence.

Overwhelmed by his contemplation, the psalmist exclaimed, "LORD, our Lord, how majestic is your name in all the earth! You have set your glory in the heavens." The whole creation is radiant and full of His resplendent glory, and no one can measure or has measured a fraction of His greatness. Take the wings of the morning and mount up to the highest heaven, and God is there in all His glory, and His name is majestic everywhere.

Yet what amazement lies in David's words, "LORD, our Lord." Despite Jehovah's magnificence and grandeur, He is also our Lord. The very name of Jehovah is royalty, and yet we are privileged to know Him as our own Lord. My Lord! No words could ever express the wonder of His majesty, and therefore it is left as a note of exclamation.

"When I consider your heavens, the work of your fingers... which you have set in place." If we could transcend the most distant star, we would find that we had only arrived at the frontier of the handiwork of God. We can only imagine discovering new galaxies with new stars and new planets even more superbly conceived than our own. How great must He be who created all that we see out of nothing and regulates and maintains the courses of the heavens with His mighty hand!

The universe rises in its totality before David, and our world, with all that is in it, shrinks into minuteness at scenes so vast and unspeakably beautiful. As David considers the splendor and harmony of creation, any thoughts of human pride begin to evaporate, and he cannot help but wonder what significance he has amid the grandness on every side of him. And so he moves past the splendors of nature and steps before the majesty of nature's Grand Designer and exclaims, "What is mankind that you are mindful of them, human beings that you care for them?" It is, no doubt, a question we have all asked at one time or another.

Are we nothing but meaningless specks when considered among all of creation? Thank God, no, not hardly. We are privileged to join David in humility and to extol the divine power and goodness, for the Lord Jehovah has opened His arms and heart to us! O the wonder of His love to allow us to call Him our Lord! And so He is. How majestic is His name in all the earth!

PSALM 16

Keep me safe, my God,
  for in you I take refuge.

I say to the Lord, "You are my Lord;
  apart from you I have no good thing."
I say of the holy people who are in the land,
  "They are the noble ones in whom is all my delight."
Those who run after other gods will suffer more and more.
  I will not pour out libations of blood to such gods
  or take up their names on my lips.

Lord, you alone are my portion and my cup;
  you make my lot secure.
The boundary lines have fallen for me in pleasant places;
  surely I have a delightful inheritance.
I will praise the Lord, who counsels me;
  even at night my heart instructs me.
I keep my eyes always on the Lord.
  With him at my right hand, I will not be shaken.

Therefore my heart is glad and my tongue rejoices;
  my body also will rest secure,
because you will not abandon me to the realm of the dead,
  nor will you let your faithful one see decay.
You make known to me the path of life;
  you will fill me with joy in your presence,
  with eternal pleasures at your right hand.

This beautiful psalm of David is a prayer for protection, that he might be surrounded and defended continually by the providence of God. "Keep me safe, my God, for in you I take refuge." The word for God here is *El*—the mighty One, the omnipotent One, our overshadowing Protector, who preserves, saves, and guards us as shepherds protect their flocks or as bodyguards surround a king.

One of the great biblical names of God is "the Watcher" or "the Preserver" of men (Job 7:20), which reflects the heavenly Father's care of our lives. To be allowed to take refuge or sanctuary in Him is a magnificent statement. It means we have committed ourselves to Him, that we have no other refuge, no other hope. We hide ourselves in Him, and we stand or fall with Him.

It is within this context that David tells us his heart is so abounding in joy that he cannot contain it. Where did this remarkable joy come from? David tells us in his own words: "I keep my eyes always on the LORD. With him at my right hand, I will not be shaken."

The Hebrew word for *always* means, "I have set the Lord before me, at one time as well as another equally." In other words, by faith David purposed to have his eye upon the Lord in every place and every circumstance, in every gathering of people and every enterprise, and in every recreation and enjoyment. He would not look away or shift his faith, hope, and trust from the Lord.

If you study the life of David, you realize he experienced seasons of abounding wealth and power as well as poverty and peril, from being celebrated as a great king to being chased as a criminal in the wilderness. Through highs and lows, through wars and peace, through hunger and cold, through friends and betrayers, and despite onslaughts driven by hatred, bitterness, and contempt, David purposed never to lose sight of God.

With love's eye set upon God, David says the Lord was always at his right hand as his Protector. This phrase of speech is used to describe those who, when they take upon themselves the care for and the defense of another person, will set that person on their right hand as the most safe place. As a child comes under the protection of his father's arms and hands during a time of imminent danger, so a person of faith is surrounded and kept by the power of God, both against present evils and dangers to come.

With the Lord at his right hand, David "will not be shaken" by anything that comes his way and will not be moved away from doing what is right. On our own, we could never stand, but by His presence and power we may prevail at all times. And when we are most severely tested and tried, He is ever ready at our right hand to keep us from falling.

PSALM 19

The heavens declare the glory of God;
   the skies proclaim the work of his hands.
Day after day they pour forth speech;
   night after night they reveal knowledge.
They have no speech, they use no words;
   no sound is heard from them.
Yet their voice goes out into all the earth,
   their words to the ends of the world.
In the heavens God has pitched a tent for the sun.
   It is like a bridegroom coming out of his chamber,
   like a champion rejoicing to run his course.
It rises at one end of the heavens
   and makes its circuit to the other;
   nothing is deprived of its warmth.

The law of the LORD is perfect,
   refreshing the soul.
The statutes of the LORD are trustworthy,
   making wise the simple.
The precepts of the LORD are right,
   giving joy to the heart.
The commands of the LORD are radiant,
   giving light to the eyes.
The fear of the LORD is pure,
   enduring forever.
The decrees of the LORD are firm,
   and all of them are righteous.

They are more precious than gold,
    than much pure gold;
they are sweeter than honey,
    than honey from the honeycomb.
By them your servant is warned;
    in keeping them there is great reward.
But who can discern their own errors?
    Forgive my hidden faults.
Keep your servant also from willful sins;
    may they not rule over me.
Then I will be blameless,
    innocent of great transgression.

May these words of my mouth
    and this meditation of my heart
    be pleasing in your sight,
    LORD, my Rock and my Redeemer.

As a young shepherd who kept his father's sheep on Bethlehem's hillsides, David devoted himself to the study of nature, which is God's common book for everyone in the world to read, and to the study of "the law of the LORD," the written Scriptures. He had so meticulously done his research on these two great books that in this psalm he is able to definitively evaluate them side by side, all the while singing the praises of the Author of both.

Nature does not hint at or whisper the glory of God—it shouts His glory, and it never stops. The heavens above will never cease to proclaim His majesty. They declare their message from day to day and from night to night. Just as one messenger quiets, another takes up his speech. These voiceless, visible messengers declare to every human being that behind all we see is a glorious God as the Maker of the world. This is His handiwork, and it reflects Him who is glorious in every way.

Nature points clearly to God and His glory as Creator. When we contemplate the heavens, what other conclusion might we reach? God speaks of Himself through the heavens in a language that anyone can hear and understand. The pale silver moon you see tonight is the same moon that shines down on Los Angeles and London and Singapore, and the same moon that Noah and Abraham enjoyed. David states that all men can be held accountable for acknowledging the truth of what nature communicates.

Yet David tells us he has found an even grander revelation of God—"the law of the LORD," the written Word of God in the Bible, which is perfect and absolute truth. It purposes to renew and revive our lives by restoring our relationship with God. Jehovah has spoken, and His Word is always right, always enlightening our minds, and always without uncertainty, compromise, or any hidden small print. It is pure because it is a clear reflection of the person and will of God, and it reveals and corrects all the wrongs, the errors, and the hidden faults of our lives.

The Word of God is like gold, even pure gold, for the spiritual treasure it brings is far more precious than any material wealth. And in keeping His Word, there is great reward—the joy of the Lord, the rest of a clear conscience, the refreshing grace and mercy of God are so precious and glorious. O to be able to live a life both in thought and word that is pleasing in God's sight! The rewards of grace are far beyond our wildest anticipations.

PSALM 23

The LORD is my shepherd, I lack nothing.
  He makes me lie down in green pastures,
he leads me beside quiet waters,
  he refreshes my soul.
He guides me along the right paths
  for his name's sake.
Even though I walk
  through the darkest valley,
I will fear no evil,
  for you are with me;
your rod and your staff,
  they comfort me.

You prepare a table before me
  in the presence of my enemies.
You anoint my head with oil;
  my cup overflows.
Surely your goodness and love will follow me
  all the days of my life,
and I will dwell in the house of the LORD
  forever.

David, the shepherd lad who became one of the most beloved kings and poets in the world's history, sings this simple yet magnificent psalm of Him who is the true Shepherd of all men. While we are uncertain whether David wrote the psalm as a young man eager for adventure or as a weary king, it conveys a maturity and an assured confidence that speaks of a faith mellowed by years of experience.

Assuming this psalm was penned during David's later years, imagine for a moment the aged king as he contemplates the green pastures, the quiet waters, and the secluded wilderness valleys where he cared for his flocks as a young man. Then move on from that lovely pastoral setting and consider David as he passes through all the following years of joy as well as overwhelming sorrow, and yet he is still able to say that during all the days of his life he has known God's goodness and love. Truly amazing!

This has been said to be the pearl of David's psalms, its soft and pure radiance charming and enriching readers and lodging deep in the treasury of many of our memories. In the simplest of words, this delightful song displays an unrivaled combination of spirituality and poetry. Century after century, it has conveyed a commonality of life experiences and shared emotions that makes it the cherished friend of people of all ages and in all places. Has any other poem ever calmed more fears or dried more tears?

"The LORD is my shepherd" may be the most beautiful sentence ever written. All of one's life fits comfortably under its cover, and the dazzling centerpiece is that little word *my*. Who would dream that the infinite Jehovah would care intimately for me and for you? David lived his life with the deep assurance that he was one of

God's sheep, and we should as well. In all of life's circumstances, it is the Shepherd who keeps the sheep, and the sheep simply trust the Shepherd with everything. He refreshes us when we are exhausted, heals us when we are diseased, and protects us with His goodness and mercy! This song will go on singing to our children and to their children, through all the generations of time . . . until we finally come to "dwell in the house of the LORD forever."

PSALM 24

The earth is the Lord's, and everything in it,
  the world, and all who live in it;
for he founded it on the seas
  and established it on the waters.

Who may ascend the mountain of the Lord?
  Who may stand in his holy place?
The one who has clean hands and a pure heart,
  who does not trust in an idol
  or swear by a false god.

They will receive blessing from the Lord
  and vindication from God their Savior.
Such is the generation of those who seek him,
  who seek your face, God of Jacob.

Lift up your heads, you gates;
  be lifted up, you ancient doors,
  that the King of glory may come in.
Who is this King of glory?
  The Lord strong and mighty,
  the Lord mighty in battle.
Lift up your head, you gates;
  lift them up, you ancient doors,
  that the King of glory may come in.
Who is he, this King of glory?
  The Lord Almighty—
  he is the King of glory.

    This psalm, a triumph song, is thought to have been composed in connection with King David's bringing of the Ark of the Covenant into Jerusalem, the citadel of Mount Zion (see 2 Samuel 6). The Ark was the most sacred object of the Israelites, having a gold cover known as "the mercy seat" as well as winged cherubim who marked the manifest presence of God within it. David sought on this historic occasion to make the people to whom he had given a capital city—and now was providing a center of divine worship—as aware of Jehovah's presence as he was.

    Imagine the long procession of white-robed priests carrying and accompanying the Ark, followed by a joyous crowd of people singing as they approached the great city, "Who may ascend the mountain of the LORD? Who may stand in his holy place?" They are asking themselves whether or not they are worthy to make this ascent. They reach the city gates, which we assume to have been closed, and from the chorus outside there resonates the directive, "Lift up your heads, you gates; be lifted up, you ancient doors, that the King of glory may come in." Then from within the walls, another choir answers with the question, "Who is this King of glory?" Triumphantly, the reply rings out, "The LORD strong and mighty, the LORD mighty in battle." Still reluctant, the question from within is raised again, "Who is he, this King of glory?" And the resounding answer is, "The LORD Almighty—he is the King of glory." At the restated declaration, the ancient gates roll back, the Ark with the divine presence enters Jerusalem, and Jehovah takes His place of rest in the city.

    Doesn't this scene portray what we all want—to have the King of glory reign and rule within our lives? But the question of the choir echoes deep in all our hearts and remains the question of all those who seek the face, the presence, of God. "Who may ascend the mountain of the LORD?" In heaven, He reigns in dazzling glory, so who on earth shall stand in His presence? Certainly, none of us on our own merits. The qualifiers—to have clean hands and a pure heart without vanity and deceit—require a divine work of grace and forgiveness in our lives, or else our faith is a delusion. The only way to "stand in his holy place" is to have received the blessing of salvation from the Lord and the righteousness that comes from God our Savior. We are first humbled by God and made to become receivers of His free gift of mercy.

To seek the Lord above everything else in life, to desire to have a clear vision of the face of God, sets us apart as a generation of our own. This may be out of character with how others want to live, but we choose to live with His name upon us as the beloved of God.

PSALM 27

The LORD is my light and my salvation—
   whom shall I fear?
The LORD is the stronghold of my life—
   of whom shall I be afraid?

When the wicked advance against me
   to devour me,
it is my enemies and my foes
   who will stumble and fall.
Though an army besiege me,
   my heart will not fear;
though war break out against me,
   even then I will be confident.

One thing I ask from the LORD,
   this only do I seek:
that I may dwell in the house of the LORD
   all the days of my life,
to gaze on the beauty of the LORD
   and to seek him in his temple.
For in the day of trouble
   he will keep me safe in his dwelling;
he will hide me in the shelter of his sacred tent
   and set me high upon a rock.

Then my head will be exalted
   above the enemies who surround me;
at his sacred tent I will sacrifice with shouts of joy;
   I will sing and make music to the LORD.

Hear my voice when I call, LORD;
   be merciful to me and answer me.
My heart says of you, "Seek his face!"
   Your face, LORD, I will seek.
Do not hide your face from me,
   do not turn your servant away in anger;
   you have been my helper.
Do not reject me or forsake me,
   God my Savior.
Though my father and mother forsake me,
   the LORD will receive me.
Teach me your way, LORD;
   lead me in a straight path
   because of my oppressors.
Do not turn me over to the desire of my foes,
   for false witnesses rise up against me,
   spouting malicious accusations.

I remain confident of this:
   I will see the goodness of the LORD
   in the land of the living.
Wait for the LORD;
   be strong and take heart
   and wait for the LORD.

The long years in David's life when he was being pursued as a fugitive by King Saul and living in caves in the wilderness are rich in psalms. This psalm bears all the marks of his wilderness meditations and should be read in that light. Imagine David standing high upon a rock, gazing down on yet another trap he has evaded and watching the soldiers of Saul searching for him among the rocks and ravines, then penning the opening words of this psalm: "The LORD is my light and my salvation—whom shall I fear?"

David lived with the rich assurance that the Lord was his personal light and salvation. First, the Lord is light and brings His light into the darkness of our lives. When He becomes our light within, He also becomes our salvation. With Him lighting us along the way of salvation, who or what need we fear? These bold words are very much reminiscent of those stated a millennium or so later by the apostle Paul in the New Testament: "If God is for us, who can be against us?" (Romans 8:31).

Given David's perilous living circumstances, we might expect that if he had one desire, it would be for a place that was absolutely safe from Saul, or for a hundred other comforts. But he tells us he has set his heart on this purpose: "One thing I ask from the LORD, this only do I seek: that I may dwell in the house of the LORD all the days of my life, to gaze on the beauty of the LORD and to seek him in his temple." Of all the things David might have desired, why this one?

The temple was called the house of God because He was manifestly present there in the Ark of the Covenant. The one thing that dominated David's thoughts and prayers was that he might dwell in a close relationship with the King, living within that sanctuary of God's presence and fellowship. Herein he could more lovingly admire God's beauty and keep looking with reverence upon God's character and glory. To seek God in His temple would allow David to converse with the Lord about all the concerns of his life.

It is a blessing that David's one purpose may be ours as well! Although the Jewish tabernacle and the temple are long gone, we may dwell in the house of the Lord all the days of our lives, for every place is God's house. The ideal for our desires and prayers is that we might be enabled to always walk consciously in God's presence, to gaze upon His beauty, and seek to know Him more.

There are many who pray or even sing David's words, but not all do so with his heart's desire. May it be our fixed purpose and resolve for every day, whether we are in our workplace, in our kitchen, or in our car, that we may dwell in the house of the Lord all the days of our lives.

PSALM 29

Ascribe to the LORD, you heavenly beings,
   ascribe to the LORD glory and strength.
Ascribe to the LORD the glory due his name;
   worship the LORD in the splendor of his holiness.

The voice of the LORD is over the waters;
   the God of glory thunders,
   the LORD thunders over the mighty waters.
The voice of the LORD is powerful;
   the voice of the LORD is majestic.
The voice of the LORD breaks the cedars;
   the LORD breaks in pieces the cedars of Lebanon.
He makes Lebanon leap like a calf,
   Sirion like a young wild ox.
The voice of the LORD strikes
   with flashes of lightning.
The voice of the LORD shakes the desert;
   the LORD shakes the Desert of Kadesh.
The voice of the LORD twists the oaks
   and strips all the forests bare.
And in his temple all cry, "Glory!"

The LORD sits enthroned over the flood;
   the LORD is enthroned as King forever.
The LORD gives strength to his people;
   the LORD blesses his people with peace.

Just as Psalm 8 is best read by moonlight under the starry sky, one should read this psalm by the flash of lightning in the roaring tempest of a thunderstorm. David describes a towering thunderstorm gathering over the Mediterranean and passing by Lebanon and along the inland mountains, reaching Jerusalem and sending the people scurrying into the temple for refuge, and finally dissolving in floods of rain. There are few phenomena in nature so awesome and violent as a thunderstorm, the sudden force of which can be so strong that the greatness of the power of the Lord is felt in heaven and on earth.

Far too often we ascribe power to natural causes, when in fact we should ascribe that power to the infinite Jehovah who is the true source of all. The Lord is to be worshipped and adored for who He is and what He does in the world, and in this case that includes what He does meteorologically, for "the LORD thunders over the mighty waters." Outside there may be thunder and lightning and wind and shaking, but our place is to always "ascribe to the LORD the glory due his name; worship the LORD in the splendor of his holiness."

These verses follow the path of the onrushing storm, and to David it is as though he hears the many voices of nature proclaiming the glory of God. Somehow, everything that seems startling and overwhelming and stirs up fearfulness and dread will lead in the end to the glory of God. Our God, David says, is easily seen everywhere, and all the earth is hushed by the majesty of His presence. Far out "over the mighty waters" and "over the flood," Jehovah is King, and He shall sit as King forever. He is calm and unshaken, however much the mighty waters may roar and be troubled. His kingdom rules the most unpredictable and uncontrollable of created things.

So wait patiently, trusting in God. Your worries and concerns are safe in His hands. In the cool calm after the storm, the grand power of God is promised to be "strength to his people." He who shakes the earth with His voice "blesses his people with peace."

Why, then, are we weak when we have divine strength at our disposal? Why are we troubled when the Lord's peace is ours? Sing this splendid psalm in whatever storm or distress hits your life. Much like how storms arise quickly and in a moment hurl down the mightiest trees, even so the Lord can bring down whatever high and imposing thing may be overshadowing your life. Sing amid whatever thunder and lightning comes your way. Strength and peace are your gift from the Lord, and surely that should set you to singing!

PSALM 32

Blessed is the one
   whose transgressions are forgiven,
   whose sins are covered.
Blessed is the one
   whose sin the Lord does not count against them
   and in whose spirit is no deceit.

When I kept silent,
   my bones wasted away
   through my groaning all day long.
For day and night
   your hand was heavy on me;
my strength was sapped
   as in the heat of summer.

Then I acknowledged my sin to you
   and did not cover up my iniquity.
I said, "I will confess
   my transgressions to the Lord."
And you forgave
   the guilt of my sin.

Therefore let all the faithful pray to you
	while you may be found;
surely the rising of the mighty waters
	will not reach them.
You are my hiding place;
	you will protect me from trouble
	and surround me with songs of deliverance.

I will instruct you and teach you in the way you should go;
	I will counsel you with my loving eye on you.
Do not be like the horse or the mule,
	which have no understanding
but must be controlled by bit and bridle
	or they will not come to you.
Many are the woes of the wicked,
	but the LORD's unfailing love
	surrounds the one who trusts in him.

Rejoice in the LORD and be glad, you righteous;
	sing, all you who are upright in heart!

This psalm, which has been a source of healing for many readers, originated from the depths of a conscience that had been deeply wounded and subsequently healed. Following a sordid affair with Bathsheba and the subsequent murder of her husband, David knew how marvelous it was to have his sins forgiven. He tried to cover his sin but found it to be a bitterness that consumed his body and soul. As long as David lived in defiance of his guilty conscience, he was miserable.

The psalm begins with David's exclamation, for its first sentence is better translated, "O blessedness is the one whose transgressions are forgiven, whose sins are covered!" There is a burst of relief and delight whenever a heart genuinely experiences the fresh joy of forgiveness. The Hebrew word *to forgive* signifies to carry out of sight or take away, as a burden is lifted or a barrier removed. The forgiven one is happy, blessed, and at peace, because life's greatest problem is solved when he or she is restored to a personal relationship with God by His free grace.

Of all the things in the world that David most prized, God's pardoning mercy is shown to be the only way to happiness. Blessedness, to know you are under the favor of God, is the most supreme and perfect of blessings. But it is not simply pronounced as the reward to those who diligently keep the laws of God. Because we all fall short of perfection, it can never come to us alone. Rather, blessedness comes to lawbreakers, who by the gift of God's grace have been freely forgiven. To have one's sins covered, hidden away forever from the sight of the all-seeing God, is amazing in the superlative!

Note the remarkable collection of statements David makes,

all expressing substantially the same thoughts about forgiveness, only with different twists. He lifts his diamond of forgiveness, as it were, into the light and slowly turns it, and with each turn it reflects the light from a different angle. All we have done that separates us from God, all we have done that is in rebellion against and takes us away from the loving heavenly Father, and all we have done that causes us to miss the mark of His destiny for our lives—to glorify God and enjoy Him forever—is no longer counted against us. This is an incomprehensible blessing.

Who is blessed? Not one who conceals and refuses to acknowledge his sin. Self-deception and hypocrisy bring no blessing. He who is pardoned has learned to be honest with himself and God about his sin. Forgiveness is authentic, and the peace that it brings is not the result of playing tricks with one's conscience. When a person has experienced forgiveness, he or she has courage of spirit to get rid of deceit and to be truthful before God, because true faith renders deceit as no longer necessary. The believer has nothing to hide, because he knows that God sees everything about him, and therefore he is free to be his true, authentic self. Free from guilt, free from deceit, free to stand up straight and walk uprightly is the reality of the person whom God forgives—blessed, indeed!

PSALM 34

I will extol the LORD at all times;
  his praise will always be on my lips.
I will glory in the LORD;
  let the afflicted hear and rejoice.
Glorify the LORD with me;
  let us exalt his name together.

I sought the LORD, and he answered me;
  he delivered me from all my fears.
Those who look to him are radiant;
  their faces are never covered with shame.
This poor man called, and the LORD heard him;
  he saved him out of all his troubles.
The angel of the LORD encamps around those who fear him,
  and he delivers them.

Taste and see that the LORD is good;
  blessed is the one who takes refuge in him.
Fear the LORD, you his holy people,
  for those who fear him lack nothing.
The lions may grow weak and hungry,
  but those who seek the LORD lack no good thing.
Come, my children, listen to me;
  I will teach you the fear of the LORD.
Whoever of you loves life
  and desires to see many good days,
keep your tongue from evil
  and your lips from telling lies.

Turn from evil and do good;
  seek peace and pursue it.

The eyes of the LORD are on the righteous,
  and his ears are attentive to their cry;
but the face of the LORD is against those who do evil,
  to blot out their name from the earth.

The righteous cry out, and the LORD hears them;
  he delivers them from all their troubles.
The LORD is close to the brokenhearted
  and saves those who are crushed in spirit.

The righteous person may have many troubles,
  but the LORD delivers him from them all;
he protects all his bones,
  not one of them will be broken.

Evil will slay the wicked;
  the foes of the righteous will be condemned.
The LORD will rescue his servants;
  no one who takes refuge in him will be condemned.

This psalm was written to commemorate David's humiliating escape from Abimelech, the Philistine king of Gath (see I Samuel 21:10–15). The Bible never hides the faults of even its greatest characters, and in this revealing situation, after David is forced to flee from the rage of King Saul, he seeks shelter in the enemy city that claimed the giant Goliath as its hero. There David's identity is quickly discovered, and he is brought before the king. Fearful for his life, and demonstrating none of the faith he had shown in defeating Goliath, David pretends to be insane. After suffering the king's contempt, he is allowed to leave with his face being "covered with shame."

In this psalm, we are given a glimpse of the lessons David learned from this experience as well as how his faith held him up despite his disgrace. Why did David fail? Because rather than looking to the Lord for help, as he did when he encountered Goliath, he focused upon the ruthlessness of men. In retrospect, David warns us not to fear the schemes of men, but rather the danger of stepping away from God's protection. We are to "fear the LORD" only, with *fear* in this context meaning reverence, awe, and respect.

The good news of the psalm is that "the eyes of the LORD are on the righteous, and his ears are attentive to their cry." The word *attentive* means that He leans toward and inclines His ears to hear even the faintest of our prayers. In fact, the Lord no sooner hears "the righteous cry out, and . . . he delivers them from all their troubles." No trouble can so hold us that the Lord cannot free us. He will show Himself strong on our behalf.

The consolation for David and for us is that "the LORD is close to the brokenhearted." Heartbreak comes in many forms. Perhaps our heart has been broken by the cruelty or the unfaithfulness of someone we loved and trusted. Or perhaps we attempted to do something that we felt was our life purpose, but when we failed, the strings of our heart were snapped.

Unfortunately, in these distressing moments we usually think God is far away, and we step back from the situation and retreat into the shadows, hoping to heal on our own. If it is dark in your life and you feel deserted, it is not so. God is with you. He will never abandon or forsake you. Call to Him as David did, for even a whisper of faith will bring a response.

"The LORD . . . saves those who are crushed in spirit." Just when we condemn ourselves for failing to live up to our convictions or for something that went wrong in our lives, the Lord graciously comes to us and forgives us, saves and delivers us from our troubles. The great Lover of our soul will always come to us as our Guardian and Friend, and He restores those who take refuge in Him. Good news for David, and good news for us!

PSALM 42

As the deer pants for streams of water,
  so my soul pants for you, my God.
My soul thirsts for God, for the living God.
  When can I go and meet with God?
My tears have been my food
  day and night,
while people say to me all day long,
  "Where is your God?"
These things I remember
  as I pour out my soul:
how I used to go to the house of God
  under the protection of the Mighty One
with shouts of joy and praise
  among the festive throng.

Why, my soul, are you downcast?
  Why so disturbed within me?
Put your hope in God,
  for I will yet praise him,
  my Savior and my God.

My soul is downcast within me;
  therefore I will remember you
from the land of the Jordan,
  the heights of Hermon—from Mount Mizar.
Deep calls to deep
  in the roar of your waterfalls;
all your waves and breakers
  have swept over me.

By day the LORD directs his love,
   at night his song is with me—
   a prayer to the God of my life.

I say to God my Rock,
   "Why have you forgotten me?
Why must I go about mourning,
   oppressed by the enemy?"
My bones suffer mortal agony
   as my foes taunt me,
saying to me all day long,
   "Where is your God?"

Why, my soul, are you downcast?
   Why so disturbed within me?
Put your hope in God,
   for I will yet praise him,
   my Savior and my God.

Can you see the exhausted deer, fleeing from the hounds, panting for the streams of water? Such was the psalmist's portrait of his life. Oppressed and taunted by his enemies, deeply discouraged and downcast emotionally to the breaking point, he cries out for the living God.

No one has to tell the thirsting deer what it needs, and the same is true for our souls when we find ourselves in David's downcast condition. To *thirst* is to be aware that one of the most basic necessities of life must be supplied immediately. For our body to thirst for water or our soul to thirst after God are perfectly natural desires. Both thirsts are divinely created in us, and when we fail to respond to either, we become weak, depleted, and in danger.

Bottom line: our heart desperately needs God, who alone has made provision for every legitimate aspiration, desire, and thirst of the soul. When we are painfully conscious of our need, we cry out to God to meet our need. Out of our emptiness, to pray, to seek the divine presence, is profoundly natural for the soul.

Unfortunately, many of us cast about to see what man-made provisions we can find to satisfy the thirst of our soul. We think that money, or drugs, or sex, or alcohol, or gaining other people's acceptance, or getting the job and the house of our dreams is the answer. Not only do these things not quench our thirst, they actually create a deeper thirst that nothing can satisfy.

Our living souls must have an all-sufficient living God or our souls will thirst and die. As Blaise Pascal said, we were created to need God and nothing less than all of God: "There is a God-shaped vacuum in the heart of every man which cannot be filled by any created thing, but only by God, the Creator." We can know the true God, living and abiding in us. If we will come to Him, He will give us the full supply of everything we need. But we must come to Him and to Him alone.

PSALM 43

Vindicate me, my God,
   and plead my cause
   against an unfaithful nation.
Rescue me from those who are
   deceitful and wicked.
You are God my stronghold.
   Why have you rejected me?
Why must I go about mourning,
   oppressed by the enemy?
Send me your light and your faithful care,
   let them lead me;
let them bring me to your holy mountain,
   to the place where you dwell.
Then I will go to the altar of God,
   to God, my joy and my delight.
I will praise God with the lyre,
   O God, my God.

Why, my soul, are you downcast?
   Why so disturbed within me?
Put your hope in God,
   for I will yet praise him,
   my Savior and my God.

Psalm 43 reads as a continuation of Psalm 42, expressing the same emotions of trouble and sorrow and, more important, the same trust in God. Three times in these two psalms, the psalmist takes himself to task for the downcast emotions that are surging in his soul, and he checks these by telling himself the truth. Specifically, he says, "Why, my soul, are you downcast? Why so disturbed within me? Put your hope in God, for I will yet praise him, my Savior and my God."

Acting as his own counselor, the psalmist talks to himself. "Why, my soul, are you downcast?" Granted, the feelings of sadness, or doubt, or worry, or confusion are the natural result of the circumstances in which he finds himself, but no matter how strong these feelings are, David tells himself that their cause is not sufficient to justify his yielding to unhappiness. "Why so disturbed within me?" His faith begins to reason with his discouragement, and his hope argues with his sadness. "If God is mine, why am I so down in the dumps? Will these present troubles last forever? Are the taunts of my foes more than empty chatter? Does my present separation from the temple worship mean I will never make it back?"

It is essential to be aware of our feelings and to keep a very tight rein upon them, lest they overwhelm us. To search out the root of the problem that is causing the feeling is the best medicine. Self-ignorance is not blissful; in David's case, it has led to misery. The gloom of not knowing the source of our negative feelings magnifies them; a little sunshine of truth will make the giants shrink into shadows.

"Put your hope in God." Just as there is need for patience, so there is ground for hope. Rise and look up by faith and know that God is unchangeable. His grace is the ground for unshaken hope, though the skies are gloomy. If everything is dark, hope still brings its own light energized by the presence of God. As surely as the sun is in the heavens, light will arise for the people of God, though for a while we may walk in darkness.

"I will yet praise him." Our sighs will give way to songs, and our somber dirges will be changed to hymns of praise. Any loss of the present sense of God's love is not a loss of that love itself. Hope knows God's promises are true even when they seem distant and dim. Times of sadness and disappointment will soon end, and seasons of praise will begin. It is time for the downcast heart to revive.

Whatever you might be going through, remember who God is—my Savior and my God. There is a wonderful calming power in repeating this amazing truth as David did. If we are assured that God is ours and that we are His, the challenges of life will be far less effective in disturbing us.

PSALM 46

God is our refuge and strength,
  an ever-present help in trouble.
Therefore we will not fear, though the earth give way
  and the mountains fall into the heart of the sea,
though its waters roar and foam
  and the mountains quake with their surging.

There is a river whose streams make glad the city of God,
  the holy place where the Most High dwells.
God is within her, she will not fall;
  God will help her at break of day.
Nations are in uproar, kingdoms fall;
  he lifts his voice, the earth melts.

The Lord Almighty is with us;
  the God of Jacob is our fortress.

Come and see what the Lord has done,
  the desolations he has brought on the earth.
He makes wars cease
  to the ends of the earth.
He breaks the bow and shatters the spear;
  he burns the shields with fire.
He says, "Be still, and know that I am God;
  I will be exalted among the nations,
  I will be exalted in the earth."

The Lord Almighty is with us;
  the God of Jacob is our fortress.

This psalm originally commemorated the supernatural deliverance of the armies of King Jehoshaphat, as described in 2 Chronicles 20. On that day, the people were told, "Do not be afraid or discouraged because of this vast army. For the battle is not yours, but God's," and as the singers went ahead of the army, singing praises to the Lord, a tremendous victory took place.

The psalmists often state that others may boast of their impregnable castles built on inaccessible rocks and secured with gates of iron, but "God is our refuge and strength," a far better refuge from distress than all of these. The psalmist declared that we boast not in our own strength, but in Jehovah, the only living and true God. Count yourself safe and say, "He is my refuge and strength." Make yourself strong in God and never forget that God is our refuge now as truly as when these words were first sung. All other refuges are counterfeit, and all other strengths are weakness, for all power belongs to God. With Him, our defense and might are equal to any circumstances we face.

Our God is "an ever-present help in trouble." He has been tried and proved by His people to be very powerful and effectual in all difficulties. He never withdraws Himself but remains present, close at our side and ready for our support, and His assistance comes at the needed time. When it is very dark with us, let brave spirits sing out these words. Such strength we have found in Him, and therefore we celebrate His praise.

"Therefore we will not fear." With God on our side, how irrational would fear be! Where He is, all power is, and all love—why therefore should we draw back? Let the worst come, the most terrible upheavals that we can imagine, "though the earth give way and the mountains fall into the heart of the sea." God remains faithful even if all of creation, including the grandest and firmest of created objects, is so shaken as to be entirely changed in utter destruction.

God is our refuge and strength—a foundational truth that we forget all too often, a precious privilege and honor that we can never overuse. In times of trouble, we show our trust and joy in Him, and make this psalm our music for our God.

PSALM 57

Have mercy on me, my God, have mercy on me,
    for in you I take refuge.
I will take refuge in the shadow of your wings
    until the disaster has passed.

I cry out to God Most High,
    to God, who vindicates me.
He sends from heaven and saves me,
    rebuking those who hotly pursue me—
    God sends forth his love and his faithfulness.

I am in the midst of lions;
    I am forced to dwell among ravenous beasts—
men whose teeth are spears and arrows,
    whose tongues are sharp swords.

Be exalted, O God, above the heavens;
    let your glory be over all the earth.

They spread a net for my feet—
    I was bowed down in distress.
They dug a pit in my path—
    but they have fallen into it themselves.

My heart, O God, is steadfast,
   my heart is steadfast;
   I will sing and make music.
Awake, my soul!
   Awake, harp and lyre!
   I will awaken the dawn.

I will praise you, LORD, among the nations;
   I will sing of you among the peoples.
For great is your love, reaching to the heavens;
   your faithfulness reaches to the skies.

Be exalted, O God, above the heavens;
   let your glory be over all the earth.

It is easy to say, "God vindicates me" and "my heart, O God, is steadfast, my heart is steadfast," when life is cruising along smoothly for us. But this psalm was written by David when everything seemed like a disaster. He was fleeing from Saul and hiding in a cave, and his enemies surrounded him like lions, pursued him with swords and spears and arrows, and set nets for his feet. Nevertheless, in the midst of great difficulty and oppression, David believes in the love of God and sings his way into confidence and joyfulness.

David tells us he steadily looked away from these difficult circumstances, focusing rather on God, the Most High, who would vindicate him and fulfill His purposes in his life. Not only would God bring deliverance, but He would also send His love and faithfulness to David. It is a marvelous thing to believe that God is literally willing to work His purpose for us, if we would only have the patience to let Him do it. Most of us insist on trying to step in and make something happen through our own strength, and we shut God out of our lives just when He is coming with the only help that will truly bring it to pass.

Before God will perform His purpose for us, we must learn, as David learned, to wait in absolute dependence upon Him. We must have a heart that is steadfast or fixed upon God—set upon waiting His time, receiving His help, and doing everything according to His way and will. A heart truly based upon God and at rest in Him is resolved to "sing and make music" and "awaken the dawn" in spite of everything that otherwise might make for tears.

The Hebrew uses the metaphor of *the heart* to cover a great deal more of the inner self than we typically do in English. By the heart, we generally mean that part of us that loves something or someone. But the Old Testament speaks of the thoughts and intents as well as the affections of the heart. When David states "my heart is steadfast," he does not merely mean that he is conscious of a steadfast love for God, but also of a fixed and settled determination and an abiding communion of thought between himself and God. He not only makes this declaration as the expression of his present experience, but he also ventures that this resolve will be his future as well.

The lesson is that our faith must be a consistent force throughout our whole lives and should not give way to the ups and downs that trouble our feelings, and especially our spiritual emotions. Unless our heart is strong and unwavering, it will never sustain the burdens that it must bear or withstand the blows that it will receive. We must have a fixed determination, a steadfast love, and a continuous realization of our dependence upon God. O for a fixed heart today!

PSALM 62

Truly my soul finds rest in God;
   my salvation comes from him.
Truly he is my rock and my salvation;
   he is my fortress, I will never be shaken.

How long will you assault me?
   Would all of you throw me down—
   this leaning wall, this tottering fence?
Surely they intend to topple me
   from my lofty place;
   they take delight in lies.
With their mouths they bless,
   but in their hearts they curse.

Yes, my soul, find rest in God;
   my hope comes from him.
Truly he is my rock and my salvation;
   he is my fortress, I will not be shaken.
My salvation and my honor depend on God;
   he is my mighty rock, my refuge.
Trust in him at all times, you people;
   pour out your hearts to him,
   for God is our refuge.

Surely the lowborn are but a breath,
 the highborn are but a lie.
If weighed on a balance, they are nothing;
 together they are only a breath.
Do not trust in extortion
 or put vain hope in stolen goods;
though your riches increase,
 do not set your heart on them.

One thing God has spoken,
 two things have I heard:
"Power belongs to you, God,
 and with you, Lord, is unfailing love";
and, "You reward everyone
 according to what they have done."

What difference does believing in God make? Does our faith only influence our lives slightly, or does it touch us at every point? David's answer is suggested in these words: "Trust in him at all times, you people; pour out your hearts to him, for God is our refuge."

Faith is not a mere nodding of the head to a belief, but requires the worshipful venture of the love of our hearts. To merely assent to God in our mind is like sitting in a ship tied to the dock; to believe in God in our heart, as the King enthroned to rule our understanding, emotions, and will, is to sail out onto the great ocean and pass over the vast waters. Faith is not occasional, but a continuous duty, an unending privilege. We should trust when we can see clearly as well as when we are utterly in the dark. Great battles of adversity have to be waged, and the very act of trust will be challenged, often daily. Impostors and disappointments frequently rise to challenge the anchors of our faith, yet God deserves our confidence at all times.

We are to pour out our hearts to God. Though He knows everything about us, He desires that we lay bare our hearts to Him. To "pour out" represents the act of presenting all the contents of our heart to God. It is as though we turn our entire soul upside down in His presence and let every secret thought, desire, motive, sorrow, and sin be poured out like salt from a saltshaker. It is to unburden our soul to the Lord and allow Him to be our most intimate confidant. He has revealed His love to us; we reveal ourselves to Him. Why hide something from Him, when we cannot actually hide it?

When we try to hide or withhold something from God, we

do so to our own hurt. To keep our inner issues and struggles to ourselves is to be locked inside our own miseries. But if we unload our hearts before God, we will obtain a refuge in Him as practical and comforting as it is encouraging.

We are to do this "at all times." Our faith in and fellowship with God should not only be unreserved but constant. Indeed, prayer was never meant to be occasional, nor can it be, by its very nature. We live by breathing continually, and our faith functions by prayer continually. The mistake we often make is to think that prayer must be formal, with prepared words spoken in a particular time and place. Our spiritual life is to be found in a simple continual conversation with God, just as natural as we breathe without thinking about it.

God, after all, is a refuge for us. Whatever He may be to others, we have a special relationship with Him; for us, He is undoubtedly a refuge. Here, then, is the best of reasons for coming to Him at all times and for all things.

PSALM 65

Praise awaits you, our God, in Zion;
    to you our vows will be fulfilled.
You who answer prayer,
    to you all people will come.
When we were overwhelmed by sins,
    you forgave our transgressions.
Blessed are those you choose
    and bring near to live in your courts!
We are filled with the good things of your house,
    of your holy temple.

You answer us with awesome and righteous deeds,
    God our Savior,
the hope of all the ends of the earth
    and of the farthest seas,
who formed the mountains by your power,
    having armed yourself with strength,
who stilled the roaring of the seas,
    the roaring of their waves,
    and the turmoil of the nations.
The whole earth is filled with awe at your wonders;
    where morning dawns, where evening fades,
    you call forth songs of joy.

You care for the land and water in it;
  you enrich it abundantly.
The streams of God are filled with water
  to provide the people with grain,
  for so you have ordained it.
You drench its furrows and level its ridges;
  you soften it with showers and bless its crops.
You crown the year with your bounty,
  and your carts overflow with abundance.
The grasslands of the wilderness overflow;
  the hills are clothed with gladness.
The meadows are covered with flocks
  and the valleys are mantled with grain;
  they shout for joy and sing.

David provides us with a delightful title for God in this psalm: "You who answer prayer." It is His name and His nature, for God not only has heard, but is now answering, and always will answer prayer, since He never changes in His attributes. It is God's nature to hear and answer prayer as truly as His nature is to be merciful and just. Every sincere prayer is as surely heard as it is offered.

Because God answers all prayer, "to you all people will come." To come to God, to draw near to Him, to adore Him, to call upon and worship Him, is the life of true faith and the invitation to all people. He never refuses any that deserves the name of prayer. As certain as God is the true God, so certain is it that none who seek Him in prayer with their whole heart will depart from Him without an answer. That is awesome news for you and for me.

One of the great reasons we come to God is that "when we were overwhelmed by sins, you forgave our transgressions." The picture suggested by the psalmist is that an outside power has so overcome and set its grip upon us that all efforts to get away from that grasp are hopeless, which is precisely what sin does in our lives. Consider for a moment the invisible grasp that a certain sin has upon us—perhaps lust, pride, dishonesty, greed, anger, envy, selfishness, or an addiction. Sin becomes our master, and there is no breaking its hold unless we get God to help us to do it.

Or consider our utter helplessness in dealing with our guilt. When we do wrong, the judge within, which we call conscience, declares three things to us: "That is wrong. You are accountable for it, and you will be punished for it." No one feels the weight of guilt without an anticipation of judgment, unless we have ignored our conscience for so long that it is seared. What are we going to do with these feelings? For centuries, men have tried in vain to rid themselves of guilt. Do we think we can remove these feelings? We can try to forget or ignore or deny or minimize or laugh at our guilt, but we are utterly powerless to lighten or shake ourselves free from it in the slightest degree.

Our sins would, but for the grace of God, prevail against us in the courts of divine justice and conscience and overcome us in the battle of life. God alone can forgive them all. They are too strong and powerful for us to deny or refute or to erase the penalties that the sins merit. Ultimately, there remains no other refuge than the mercy and grace of God. What a comfort that the sins that overwhelm us do not overwhelm God. They would keep us away from God, but He sweeps them away from before Himself and us. They are too strong for us, but not for our Redeemer, who is mighty to save.

PSALM 84

How lovely is your dwelling place,
   Lord Almighty!
My soul yearns, even faints,
   for the courts of the Lord;
my heart and my flesh cry out
   for the living God.
Even the sparrow has found a home,
   and the swallow a nest for herself,
   where she may have her young—
a place near your altar,
   Lord Almighty, my King and my God.
Blessed are those who dwell in your house;
   they are ever praising you.

Blessed are those whose strength is in you,
   whose hearts are set on pilgrimage.
As they pass through the Valley of Baka,
   they make it a place of springs;
   the autumn rains also cover it with pools.
They go from strength to strength,
   till each appears before God in Zion.

Hear my prayer, Lord God Almighty;
  listen to me, God of Jacob.
Look on our shield, O God;
  look with favor on your anointed one.

Better is one day in your courts
  than a thousand elsewhere;
I would rather be a doorkeeper in the house of my God
  than dwell in the tents of the wicked.
For the Lord God is a sun and shield;
  the Lord bestows favor and honor;
no good thing does he withhold
  from those whose walk is blameless.

Lord Almighty,
  blessed is the one who trusts in you.

Pilgrimages to the temple to meet with the living God, as described in this psalm, were a grand feature of Jewish life. Families journeyed together to the feasts in Jerusalem from every corner of the land, making celebratory groups that swelled in number at each resting place. According to the psalmist, they made the pathways over the hills and through the marshes ring with their songs, creating pleasant memories that would never be forgotten.

Having spoken of the blessedness of those who dwell in God's house, the psalmist speaks longingly of those who go on the pilgrimage: "Blessed are those whose strength is in you, whose hearts are set on pilgrimage" or "in whose heart are the ways." Note that no blessing is being offered to half-hearted worshippers, but to those who throw all their energies into it. If they have left their hearts at home, neither their prayers nor their praise nor the hearing of the Word of God will bless or be pleasant to them. Only those who love the ways of God and are pressing nearer and nearer to Him, the infinite Source of all blessedness, are blessed. When we have allowed God's ways to come into our hearts, and our hearts love His ways, we become the person He desires us to be, and we enjoy His blessing and favor.

Traveling joyfully on the road to the dwelling place of the Lord Almighty, "as they pass through the Valley of Baka, they make it a place of springs; the autumn rains also cover it with pools." Baka derives from the Hebrew "to weep." Even in the Valley of Tears, so to speak, the tears of the pilgrims transformed sadness and grief into a spring of blessing, just as the early rains of autumn restored water to the valley. There are joys of the pilgrimage that make the travelers forget the trials of the road. God provides His people all they need when they walk the roads under His direction.

If the desire of our heart is to get closer to God, then even our sorrows and our tears, as we face disappointments, anxieties, and losses, both small and great, will become sources of refreshment. How different all our troubles look when we take as our great pursuit in life the great purpose that we sense God has given for us, which is to be changed into His likeness and transformed by His presence in our lives.

"They go from strength to strength, till each appears before God in Zion." Rather than being weakened by the journey or turned back in the Valley of Tears, the pilgrims are invigorated as they proceed. If getting closer to God and becoming more like Him is our goal, we grow stronger as we advance. For those who follow His ways, "better is one day in [his] courts than a thousand elsewhere." At the end of the pilgrim's march, we receive the delight of our hearts—to appear before God!

PSALM 91

Whoever dwells in the shelter of the Most High
    will rest in the shadow of the Almighty.
I will say of the LORD, "He is my refuge and my fortress,
    my God, in whom I trust."

Surely he will save you
    from the fowler's snare
    and from the deadly pestilence.
He will cover you with his feathers,
    and under his wings you will find refuge;
    his faithfulness will be your shield and rampart.
You will not fear the terror of night,
    nor the arrow that flies by day,
nor the pestilence that stalks in the darkness,
    nor the plague that destroys at midday.
A thousand may fall at your side,
    ten thousand at your right hand,
    but it will not come near you.
You will only observe with your eyes
    and see the punishment of the wicked.

If you say, "The Lord is my refuge,"
  and you make the Most High your dwelling,
no harm will overtake you,
  no disaster will come near your tent.
For he will command his angels concerning you
  to guard you in all your ways;
they will lift you up in their hands,
  so that you will not strike your foot against a stone.
You will tread on the lion and the cobra;
  you will trample the great lion and the serpent.

"Because he loves me," says the Lord, "I will rescue him;
  I will protect him, for he acknowledges my name.
He will call on me, and I will answer him;
  I will be with him in trouble,
  I will deliver him and honor him.
With long life I will satisfy him
  and show him my salvation."

Deuteronomy 32:10–11 offers the magnificent image of God's protection as that of the eagle that stirs up its nest, hovers over the young, and carries them on its wings. That passage may possibly have touched the imagination of this psalmist, when he writes: "He will cover you with his feathers, and under his wings you will find refuge; his faithfulness will be your shield and rampart."

The image of God's covering wings suggests not only protection from predators but also of nurturing, of downy warmth, of delightful closeness to the heart of God that beats with parental love, and a host of other privileges realized only by those who nestle beneath His wing. Who does not see God's matchless love and divine tenderness, which should both call to and win our confidence? Even as a hen covers her chicks, so does the Lord protect those who dwell in Him. Birds of prey and snares in the field are equally harmless when we draw close to the Lord.

This does not mean that we are spared from the calamities and disasters and temptations that fall upon other people. Many of the psalmists speak of being overwhelmed by their difficult life circumstances. Divine protection is to be understood by faith. It is a deliverance from the evil attached to the circumstance, in which the poison is, as it were, wiped off the arrow. The sorrows and sufferings come and wring our hearts as they do to others, but in our lives they are caused by God's grace to work for our good. The protection consists not in avoiding the blows, but in changing their character. For those who dwell consciously in God's presence, that protection is magnificently secure.

To find covering under His wings is a picturesque way of defining our faith—its very essence, its basic necessity, and its true worth. It speaks eloquently to us of the dangers that surround us. Yet there are many who know about the promise of God's refuge but never come under it. Faith involves our entire being, our whole person, diving beneath the shadow of His wings to take shelter. The power of faith is that it joins our heart to God's and sets us beneath the Almighty's protection. But unless we do that, we are exposed to all that this psalm warns against.

Wonderfully, God's faithfulness becomes our "shield"—not the small, light shield that an ancient warrior would bear upon his left arm, but the large shield, planted in the ground in front of him, covering and encircling him like a wall or rampart of iron. God is faithful to His Word and all that He has promised. Let us seek the refuge of His wings, and may our faith correspond to the faithfulness of Him who has promised it.

PSALM 92

It is good to praise the Lord
    and make music to your name, O Most High,
proclaiming your love in the morning
    and your faithfulness at night,
to the music of the ten-stringed lyre
    and the melody of the harp.

For you make me glad by your deeds, Lord;
    I sing for joy at what your hands have done.
How great are your works, Lord,
    how profound are your thoughts!
Senseless people do not know,
    fools do not understand,
that though the wicked spring up like grass
    and all evildoers flourish,
      they will be destroyed forever.

But you, Lord, are forever exalted.

For surely your enemies, Lord,
　　surely your enemies will perish;
　　all evildoers will be scattered.
You have exalted my horn like that of a wild ox;
　　fine oils have been poured on me.
My eyes have seen the defeat of my adversaries;
　　my ears have heard the rout of my wicked foes.

The righteous will flourish like a palm tree,
　　they will grow like a cedar of Lebanon;
planted in the house of the Lord,
　　they will flourish in the courts of our God.
They will still bear fruit in old age,
　　they will stay fresh and green,
proclaiming, "The Lord is upright;
　　he is my Rock, and there is no wickedness in him."

The psalmist tells us "it is good to praise the LORD and make music to your name, O Most High." To give thanks to God is but a small return for the phenomenal benefits that He showers upon us daily. Praise is beneficial for our heart and soul, because praise is the powerful lever that lifts and bears away the weight and shame of sin. And to sing and give God thanks inspires others to do the same. Heartfelt praise, appropriately offered, is always good and never out of season.

It is especially good for us to express our gratitude to God in song. Silent worship has its place, but vocal worship is even better. To withhold your voice from the privilege of declaring the praises of God involves shutting down one of the most natural and noble yearnings of the soul. To make music to the Most High God with our whole person is so intrinsic a part of our worship that anything less is unnatural. The Scriptures tell us the trees of the forest sing (1 Chronicles 16:33), the meadows and valleys shout and sing (Psalm 65:13), and the mountains and forests sing (Isaiah 44:23)—and they all do so for joy! Singing is also shown to be the music of God's people—as appointed daily in the temple worship, in times of great distress, in times of deliverance, and in times of abundance. And singing is the music of the angels (Job 38:7).

It is good to be "proclaiming your love in the morning." Each day is a new beginning to fill with faith and hope, and there is a freshness and charm about early morning praises. No hour is too early to begin with our best expressions of love to the throne of God's grace. Someone has said, "The day is loveliest when it first opens its eyelids, and our hearts are engrossed with the adoration of the love of God." What a privilege and honor to take our place and join the choir who ceaselessly worship the Eternal One!

And it is good "to proclaim . . . your faithfulness at night." Just as our day begins with praise, so should our day end. Every night—whether our day has been wonderful or difficult—is the appropriate time to proclaim God's faithfulness in song, since under all circumstances, it remains the same and is the foundation of all our comforts.

PSALM 93

The LORD reigns, he is robed in majesty;
  the Lord is robed in majesty and armed with strength;
  indeed, the world is established, firm and secure.
Your throne was established long ago;
  you are from all eternity.

The seas have lifted up, LORD,
  the seas have lifted up their voice;
  the seas have lifted up their pounding waves.
Mightier than the thunder of the great waters,
  mightier than the breakers of the sea—
  the LORD on high is mighty.

Your statutes, LORD, stand firm;
  holiness adorns your house
  for endless days.

There are times when troubles come our way, in unrelenting waves that surge and break against our lives with crushing force. Perhaps the psalmist had been out in a boat as a sudden windstorm battered the often stormy Sea of Galilee or watched gale-force winds bring huge waves thundering in from the Mediterranean Sea against the western coast of Philistia and Israel. If you've ever experienced the combination of high winds and high seas, you know that the voice of the ocean can be so deafening that you cannot hear yourself speak.

In the Bible, the sea is used often to represent an ungoverned force that impacts our lives, especially that of humanity in turmoil and opposition to God. It is a fitting description of how problems can rise unexpectedly around our lives, swelling and rolling over us without mercy. Caught in the waves, one can feel overwhelmed, devastated, and at times utterly beaten down.

Yet above life's storms we hear the psalmist's transcendent chorus, "Mightier than the thunder of the great waters, mightier than the breakers of the sea—the LORD on high is mighty." He who sits in heaven over the fathomless depths of the seas is the King. The mightiest wave does not shake His secure throne. Such was the psalmist's faith as he looked over his troubled world.

So what should we do when we find ourselves threatened by seas of difficulty or injustice or anxiety? Do what the psalmist did—look up at God's throne and declare that our God reigns. Too often we are so fixated on the high seas that we don't look high enough, and consequently we don't see God. We see the waves mounting higher and higher and hear the roar, but we don't lift up our eyes by faith and see the eternal throne of God.

Whatever problems or opposition may arise in our lives, He is never caught off guard. Our God has reigned, still reigns today, and will reign forever and ever.

"The LORD reigns, he is robed with majesty." What can boost our courage more than the sight of the King clothed with beauty and majesty? Not with outward symbols of majesty, but with a majesty that is intrinsic to His being. His does not resemble sovereignty; He is the embodiment of all sovereignty. "The LORD is armed with strength." Strength always dwells in the Lord Jehovah, and He proves His power by taming and calming the seas by His might. His whisper of "Seas . . . be still" is enough to silence the greatest storm and turn the wave-swept chaos into a sea of tranquility.

Therefore look above the seas of your distress and behold your King. The troubles may rise above your strength, but not above God's help; the schemes formed against you may surpass your understanding, but not the wisdom and power of God that is with you. Learn to trust God in your difficulties. The storm will not last forever. Yet, while it rages, hold tight to the Lord's promises of love and faithfulness. Our God reigns! Hallelujah!

PSALM 98

Sing to the LORD a new song,
　for he has done marvelous things;
his right hand and his holy arm
　have worked salvation for him.
The LORD has made his salvation known
　and revealed his righteousness to the nations.
He has remembered his love
　and his faithfulness to Israel;
all the ends of the earth have seen
　the salvation of our God.

Shout for joy to the LORD, all the earth,
　burst into jubilant song with music;
make music to the LORD with the harp,
　with the harp and the sound of singing,
with trumpets and the blast of the ram's horn—
　shout for joy before the LORD, the King.

Let the sea resound, and everything in it,
　the world, and all who live in it.
Let the rivers clap their hands,
　let the mountains sing together for joy;
let them sing before the LORD,
　for he comes to judge the earth.
He will judge the world in righteousness,
　and the peoples with equity.

The great invitation of the Book of Psalms is that we share not only the psalmists' faith, but we also join their choir "and sing to the LORD a new song." Far too often our daily songs are somber minor chords of loss and disappointment, of regret and shame. It is time, as the Old Testament prophet Isaiah said, "to put on the garment of praise for the spirit of heaviness." As God's amazing mercy toward us is new every morning, so our praise should be new every morning and worthy of His name. Has He not done, is He not doing, marvelous new things in our lives? Should our worship be any less?

The song of God's redeeming grace will never grow old, even though we may repeat the same words. Sing and shout about His victories, about His salvation, and about His coming to judge the earth. Listen to the rising harmonies of the seas, the rivers, and the hills; they show us how to sing and worship. The psalmist looked around creation and gave a shout of joy to the Lord, and all that was within him broke forth into a melody of thanksgiving. Eyes of faith constantly discover new and wonderful examples of God's wisdom and grace, which can only prompt new songs to make music to the Lord.

While this stirring psalm may have been written on the occasion of a great national triumph, some commentators also say it is a prophetic psalm that speaks of the coming of the Messiah, Jesus Christ, and what is here foretold is conspicuously parallel to the Magnificat, the blessed Virgin Mary's song of praise when she was greeted by her cousin Elizabeth before the birth of Christ as recorded in the Gospel of Luke (1:46–55). It would seem as though Mary had this psalm in front of her when she composed her marvelous song of triumph.

If the victory celebrated in this psalm is prophetical, it is truly a new song, a song the world had never heard until Christ's birth and the singing of the splendid angels: "Glory to God in the highest heaven, and on earth peace to those on whom his favor rests" (Luke 2:14). "Today in the town of David a Savior has been born to you; he is Messiah, the Lord" is a brand-new song that is sung by millions!

PSALM 100

Shout for joy to the LORD, all the earth.
  Worship the LORD with gladness;
  come before him with joyful songs.
Know that the LORD is God.
  It is he who made us, and we are his;
  we are his people, the sheep of his pasture.

Enter his gates with thanksgiving
  and his courts with praise;
  give thanks to him and praise his name.
For the LORD is good and his love endures forever;
  his faithfulness continues through all generations.

Why do we worship God? In this beautiful psalm, we discover that the true basis for our worship is the simple fact that God, as our Creator, owns our lives. He has an undisputable right to us and to our worship because He has made us. Before we can freely give Him the worship for which He is worthy, we must embrace His right to our lives and experience the privilege of what it means to belong to Him.

If we are to shout to the Lord for joy and worship Him with gladness and joyful sounds, the psalmist tells us that it all begins with what we understand: "Know that the LORD is God." How can you worship God if you don't know Him or the reasons why He is worthy of worship? "Man, know thyself" is ancient wisdom, but can we truly know ourselves until we know our God and what He has to say about us? Jehovah is God in the fullest, most absolute sense—He is God alone. Yet we are invited to know Him as our personal Creator, and then based on that knowledge to live our lives within His courts with thanks and praise and love.

To truly know God, to live in a personal relationship with Him, is the spring out of which our love and devotion and obedience flow. Repeatedly in the Bible God makes it clear that sacrifices and offerings are only pleasing to Him when they come from hearts filled with love and reverence. If we focus our lives on knowing Him every day, we will find our worship of Him to be more consistent and spontaneous. Only those who in daily practice "know that the LORD is God" offer praise to Him that brings pleasure to His heart.

"It is he who made us, and we are his." The prophet Isaiah

states that the Lord has made us as a potter fashions the clay for a defined purpose. Reason tells us that the divine Potter has a right to use the vessels He makes for whatever purposes He has designed for them. He has made us as the weaver puts his energies and time and skill into the making of fine linen. Reason tells us that the divine Weaver has the right to use the fabric He makes for whatever He desires. Doesn't reason also tell us that we should so esteem our Maker with our lives?

Unfortunately, most of us are taught that we must be "self-made" men and women, and we spend the majority of our lives attempting to be our own creators. By failing to recognize the true origin of our being, we are left on our own to find our way in the world.

Far better to know that we belong to the Good Shepherd: "We are his people, the sheep of his pasture." It is our honor to have been chosen to be His own people. And as sheep gather around their shepherd and look to him to be guided by his wisdom, tended by his loving care, and provided for through his abundance, we gather around the great Shepherd of mankind in the same manner. Let us enter His gates with our highest adoration for His goodness and love and faithfulness, for the simple truth is that we belong to Him.

PSALM 103

Praise the LORD, my soul;
    all my inmost being, praise his holy name.
Praise the LORD, my soul,
    and forget not all his benefits—
who forgives all your sins
    and heals all your diseases,
who redeems your life from the pit
    and crowns you with love and compassion,
who satisfies your desires with good things
    so that their youth is renewed like the eagle's.

The LORD works righteousness
    and justice for all the oppressed.

He made known his ways to Moses,
    his deeds to the people of Israel:
The LORD is compassionate and gracious,
    slow to anger, abounding in love.
He will not always accuse,
    nor will he harbor his anger forever;
he does not treat us as our sins deserve
    or repay us according to our iniquities.
For as high as the heavens are above the earth,
    so great is his love for those who fear him;
as far as the east is from the west,
    so far has he removed our transgressions from us.

As a father has compassion on his children,
    so the LORD has compassion on those who fear him;
for he knows how we are formed,
    he remembers that we are dust.
The life of mortals is like grass,
    they flourish like a flower of the field;
the wind blows over it and it is gone,
    and its place remembers it no more.
But from everlasting to everlasting
    the LORD's love is with those who fear him,
    and his righteousness with their children's children—
with those who keep his covenant
    and remember to obey his precepts.

The LORD has established his throne in heaven,
    and his kingdom rules over all.

Praise the LORD, you his angels,
    you mighty ones who do his bidding,
    who obey his word.
Praise the LORD, all his heavenly hosts,
    you his servants who do his will.
Praise the LORD, all his works
    everywhere in his dominion.

Praise the LORD, my soul.

While we know it's true that Jehovah is worthy of our highest and constant praise, we also know from experience how easy it is to begin to take Him for granted and grow half-hearted in our praise. Perhaps that's what motivated the psalmist to command his inmost being to bless the Lord with the exhortation: "Praise the LORD, my soul." The only way for us to be consistently engaged in worship is to willfully stir up our heart and whole being to it.

We need to consider what it means to daily mandate ourselves, "All my inmost being, praise his holy name," because it is easy to overlook the extent of the psalmist's all. Our inmost being includes all of our vast inner senses, emotions, and faculties, which are all designed to join in the chorus to His praise. That means our thoughts can praise him by thinking on whatever is true, right, excellent, or praiseworthy. Our conscience can praise Him by being in alignment with God's Word. Our desires can praise Him by wanting the things that God wants for us. Our memories can praise Him by putting regrets behind us and focusing on all God has provided for us. Our imaginations can praise Him by opening our minds to all He wants to do in our lives. Our will can praise Him by being faithful to act in accordance with His will.

To praise God and to love God as the only Being worthy of our highest adoration involves all of our heart, all of our soul, all of our strength, and all of our passions. It is to humbly acknowledge God for all that He is in His divine greatness and to praise Him for all the magnificent attributes—His compassion, His grace, His abounding love, His forgiveness, and His healing—that are so evidently directed toward us. It is to acknowledge our eternal debt for all we have received from Him and to bless Him with songs of praise that rise from hearts overflowing with gratitude.

"And forget not all his benefits." This touches the hidden spot of so much of our ingratitude—our forgetfulness, our failure to recall all the ways God's mercy has been poured out upon us. Why is it that our memory is so poor in recounting what God has done in our lives? We seem to have instant recall of the rubbish of our past and the bad things that have happened, while we fail to remember the priceless wonders of God's grace. The Lord forgives all our sins, has saved us with a great salvation, heals all our diseases, crowns us with love and compassion, and satisfies our desires with good things. How is it possible that praise is not continually in our hearts and on our lips? "All of his benefits"—all of them call out to us as melodies for praise and should never be taken for granted. God's all necessitates our all. Praise the Lord, my soul.

PSALM 112

Praise the LORD.

Blessed are those who fear the LORD,
    who find great delight in his commands.

Their children will be mighty in the land;
    the generation of the upright will be blessed.
Wealth and riches are in their houses,
    and their righteousness endures forever.
Even in darkness light dawns for the upright,
    for those who are gracious and compassionate and righteous.
Good will come to those who are generous and lend freely,
    who conduct their affairs with justice.

Surely the righteous will never be shaken;
    they will be remembered forever.
They will have no fear of bad news;
    their hearts are steadfast, trusting in the LORD.
Their hearts are secure, they will have no fear;
    in the end they will look in triumph on their foes.
They have freely scattered their gifts to the poor,
    their righteousness endures forever;
    their horn will be lifted high in honor.

The wicked will see and be vexed,
    they will gnash their teeth and waste away;
    the longings of the wicked will come to nothing.

Bad news seems to be the dominant theme of our times. It is constantly pouring into our lives, and the fears that accompany it are alarming. Job losses, home foreclosures, declining property values, higher taxes, credit card debt, corporate bankruptcies, earthquakes and fires: on and on goes the list.

Faith is the one antidote for all the bad news that comes our way. The psalmist tells us that one of the remarkable blessings of being a man or woman who fears the Lord is that "they will have no fear of bad news; their hearts are steadfast, trusting in the LORD. Their hearts are secure, they will have no fear." That is an amazing claim: no fear.

The life of faith is not one where we confront bad news by grabbing on to this or that biblical promise or inspirational thought and desperately trying to believe it; rather, it is to have a daily unwavering trust in our God, a quiet confidence that meets the vagaries of life. Let the future bring what it may, our God is the Lord of tomorrow. Whatever may have happened in the past, our God was not caught off guard and can help us deal with the repercussions. If the very worst should happen today, we are determined to trust the Lord. Come what may, nothing will be able to separate us from His love.

The psalmist boldly declares that to have a heart that is steadfast or fixed is to have no fear that bad news will come, and if it does come, we will be without distress. This requires that our confidence in God is established and firm; our courage is anchored in a secure foundation and supported by the power of God. With the love of God in our heart, we are ready to face any circumstance with a brave faith.

A heart that has established its confidence in God is kept in an amazing place of composure. If we hear of bad news, we can say as Job did, "The LORD gave and the LORD has taken away; may the name of the LORD be praised" (Job 1:21). The integrity of Job's faith did not rise and fall with his life circumstances, but his heart was fixed, trusting in the Lord for what He allows. His life reflected the great God whom he trusted, and in the midst of the best and the worst that life brings, he was at peace and composed, declaring to those around him that they should always worship God.

This does not mean Job did not suffer anguish and pains, or that we do not as well. Far from it. But we refuse to judge things by their appearance. If what seems like the worst thing should come, we know that God is working all things together for our good. In whatever we don't understand, we look for and trust in our Father's hand. Our heart dares to remain quiet and patient as we wait for the salvation of God.

PSALM 119

How can a young person stay on the path of purity?
    By living according to your word.
I seek you with all my heart;
    do not let me stray from your commands.
I have hidden your word in my heart
    that I might not sin against you.
Praise be to you, LORD;
    teach me your decrees.
With my lips I recount
    all the laws that come from your mouth.
I rejoice in following your statutes
    as one rejoices in great riches.
I meditate on your precepts
    and consider your ways.
I delight in your decrees;
    I will not neglect your word.

With so much uncertainty in the world today, young people face more questions about their future than ever. Many parents and educators place a tremendous emphasis on what a young person is going to do with his life and how he is preparing to achieve his goals. It is only natural to put high priority on what will lead to a happy and fulfilled life. On the other hand, many young people grow up without any plans at all, wandering aimlessly into adulthood, drifting from this to that, often struggling to make a living rather than living with a sense of purpose.

Most young people are never challenged to explore the underlying principles and values upon which their lives should be based. With so many other unsettled issues demanding attention, very few ask themselves the psalmist's crucial question: "How can a young person stay on the path of purity?" Despite society's indifference to morality, purity of heart is the best thing— purity of motives, of intentions, of will, of transparency, of truthfulness; and to first be a person of integrity, a good person, is the wisest of life's priorities.

Purity is a tremendously important issue for every person, and especially for young people. As a general rule, a young person is lacking in experience and knowledge, tends to be careless, presumptuous, and overconfident, and is often swayed by raging hormones. How will he discover what God values and live in God's way? This is the most important question anyone faces, and the best time to answer it is when we are young.

The psalmist tells us that we must try to measure every day's actions "by living according to your word"—the standard of the Word of God. Take your life and put it alongside the truths and principles of God. Cultivate the habit of bringing all that you do and all that you are side by side with this light; not only does His Word expose those areas of our lives where we miss His mark, but it also shows us the way to make it right and be transformed by His power.

There is no safeguard more effective in keeping our lives close to God than the consistent prayerful reading of the Word of God. It will shine its light on every proposition from society or from our friends, every whispered suggestion from our own hearts and passions. Asking ourselves the simple question, "What does the Bible say?" may actually keep us from ruining our lives.

PSALM 121

I lift up my eyes to the mountains—
   where does my help come from?
My help comes from the LORD,
   the Maker of heaven and earth.

He will not let your foot slip—
   he who watches over you and will not slumber;
indeed, he who watches over Israel
   will neither slumber nor sleep.

The LORD watches over you—
   the LORD is your shade at your right hand;
the sun will not harm you by day,
   nor the moon by night.

The LORD will keep you from all harm—
   he will watch over your life;
the LORD will watch over your coming and going
   both now and forevermore.

The Songs of Ascents, of which this psalm is one, may have been pilgrim psalms sung by those who were going up to celebrate the great seasonal feasts in Jerusalem. Some scholars also attribute these psalms to the time many of the Jewish people were taken in captivity to the country of Babylon (around 586 BC). We see the exiled psalmist gazing out over the endlessly flat plains of Babylonia while imagining the distant mountains of Jerusalem, where his home and place of worship had been. We hear him say to himself, "I will lift up my eyes above these dreary lowlands and look to the sacred hills that I cannot see but that I know to always be there for me."

Help comes to us only from above—from our God; we look elsewhere in vain. Let us lift up our eyes with hope, expectancy, desire, and confidence. But we will never see Him unless we choose to lift our eyes by faith. It is far easier to simply look at what is in front of us than to gaze up at the stars. Unless we strive to maintain an attitude of lifting our eyes to see God, the busyness and the burdens of life will be too much for us and down will go our gaze, and with it will go our desires for God and our aspirations for ourselves.

It is God's faithfulness we must rely upon. Whenever our focus is upon ourselves, we find nothing that lifts us up and gives us the courage to fight the battles of life. If we lose sight of where our help comes from, we are left with our fears, our disappointments, our regrets, our sins, and our lacks, which only lead toward despair. We must always find a way to lift our eyes above the swampy flats of our own unworthiness and gaze upon the hills of God.

Gazing upward by faith, no doubt wondering if he would ever be able to return to his homeland and place of worship, the psalmist states in hopeful assurance that his effort is not in vain. "My help comes from the LORD, the Maker of heaven and earth."

We will never come to receive the divine help we need in life unless we recognize that we need His help. God cannot help us until we come to the point of realizing that He is our only help. What we need is our Maker's help—powerful, operative, and constant—to keep our feet from slipping, to keep us from harm, and to watch over us. Our hope is in Jehovah, for our help comes from Him. No matter where we are, help is on the way and will not fail to reach us when we need it. Our God, who created all things, is our infinite Helper and more than equal to every situation.

Therefore let us be joyful and lift our eyes from the mundane things of life that we can see to the Maker of heaven and earth whom we cannot see. Help is ours!

PSALM 130

Out of the depths I cry to you, Lord;
  Lord, hear my voice.
Let your ears be attentive
  to my cry for mercy.

If you, Lord, kept a record of sins,
  Lord, who could stand?
But with you there is forgiveness,
  so that we can, with reverence, serve you.

I wait for the Lord, my whole being waits,
  and in his word I put my hope.
I wait for the Lord
  more than watchmen wait for the morning,
  more than watchmen wait for the morning.

Israel, put your hope in the Lord,
  for with the Lord is unfailing love
  and with him is full redemption.
He himself will redeem Israel
  from all their sins.

"Out of the depths I cry to you, Lord." Most of us know from personal experience into what depths we can sink, for any number of reasons—perhaps through sickness, or through financial distress, or in sorrow, or through depression. But the worst depth into which our soul can descend is sin. Sometimes it begins with what seems small and insignificant—with a lie or resentment or jealousy or lust or cheating or a drink—that leads down and down to greater depths. It is sin that breaks our relationship with God and does untold damage to our own lives and often to that of others as well. For some, there seems to be no bottom to the depths into which they fall.

Trapped under this sense of sin, what could the psalmist do but cry out that the Lord might hear his voice and grant him mercy? "If you, Lord, kept a record of sins, Lord, who could stand?" If Jehovah, the all-seeing One, were to call us to answer for every lack of conformity to His righteousness, what would we do? Who could stand before the Lord's throne, before the great King of holiness and purity, and hope to be pronounced as accepted? No one can answer for himself before a Judge so perfect, concerning a law so divine. Assuredly, our thoughts and words and acts convict us.

Thank God, there is free, full, sovereign forgiveness in the hand of the great King! It is His right to pardon, and He delights to exercise it. Because His nature is mercy, and because He has provided a sacrifice for sin, forgiveness is with Him for all who come to Him confessing their sins. The power of divine pardon is available at this moment, and when God once declares forgiveness, it can never be undone.

The fountain of God's forgiveness springs perpetually from His heart. Receive it and be thankful. You may not experience a rush of emotion, but dare to believe that your prayers and confessions have been heard and answered. Fear and doubt and questions may linger, but they cannot annul the forgiveness of God. Stand upon it as a fact.

"But with you there is forgiveness, so that we can, with reverence, serve you." Gratitude for pardon produces far more fear, or reverence, of God than all the dread that accompanies the thought of punishment. No one reverences the Lord as much as those who have experienced His forgiving love. This forgiveness, this smile of God, binds our soul to God with a beautiful awe and reverence. Our privilege, then, is to drink deep of God's forgiving love until we are filled with eternal hope.

You have searched me, LORD,
  and you know me.
You know when I sit and when I rise;
  you perceive my thoughts from afar.
You discern my going out and my lying down;
  you are familiar with all my ways.
Before a word is on my tongue
  you, LORD, know it completely.
You hem me in behind and before,
  and you lay your hand upon me.
Such knowledge is too wonderful for me,
  too lofty for me to attain.

Where can I go from your Spirit?
  Where can I flee from your presence?
If I go up to the heavens, you are there;
  if I make my bed in the depths, you are there.
If I rise on the wings of the dawn,
  if I settle on the far side of the sea,
even there your hand will guide me,
  your right hand will hold me fast.
If I say, "Surely the darkness will hide me
  and the light become night around me,"
even the darkness will not be dark to you;
  the night will shine like the day,
  for darkness is as light to you.

For you created my inmost being;
 you knit me together in my mother's womb.
I praise you because I am fearfully and wonderfully made;
 your works are wonderful,
 I know that full well.
My frame was not hidden from you
 when I was made in the secret place,
 when I was woven together in the depths of the earth.
Your eyes saw my unformed body;
 all the days ordained for me were written in your book
 before one of them came to be.
How precious to me are your thoughts, God!
 How vast is the sum of them!
Were I to count them,
 they would outnumber the grains of sand—
 when I awake, I am still with you.

If only you, God, would slay the wicked!
 Away from me, you who are bloodthirsty!
They speak of you with evil intent;
 your adversaries misuse your name.
Do I not hate those who hate you, LORD,
 and abhor those who are in rebellion against you?
I have nothing but hatred for them;
 I count them my enemies.
Search me, God, and know my heart;
 test me and know my anxious thoughts.
See if there is any offensive way in me,
 and lead me into the way everlasting.

Did you ever wonder how a young shepherd who became a world-renowned warrior and king could compose this psalm, which is perhaps the grandest reflection of the all-knowing God that has ever been put into words? Magnificently, David bypasses all the generalities and clichés regarding God's power, and he instead focuses on the wonder of God in his own life: "You have searched me, Lord, and you know me." "Such knowledge," David says of the intimate relationship God has with him, "is too wonderful for me"—it takes his breath away.

"Search me, God" is a prayer born of a confident love. The word *search* is a picturesque one, meaning to "dig deep." God is asked, as it were, to cut into David and expose his inmost nature. "Search me"—dig into me, bring the deepest parts to light, turn me inside out—"and know my heart"—the center of my personality, my inmost self. God's infallible knowledge of us is welcome because His heart is pure love. There is a blessed joy in discovering ourselves, even our unworthy selves, when we know that the infinite Lover of our hearts also desires to purify our hearts.

"See if there is any offensive way in me." We all have such ways deeply lodged within us—some we are aware of, and others we are not. But if we will turn ourselves to Him, He will expose our faults and show us what is wrong. One of the characteristics of sin is to get us to hide from God and to keep us from knowing our true condition. Every child of God will desire, even if it is painful, to know his heart as God knows it, in order that he might be delivered from any offenses altogether.

The "offensive way" is in us by nature; we need to be led by the divine hand into the "way everlasting." O to be led in the paths of right living and everlasting life!

PSALM 145

I will exalt you, my God the King;
   I will praise your name for ever and ever.
Every day I will praise you
   and extol your name for ever and ever.

Great is the LORD and most worthy of praise;
   his greatness no one can fathom.
One generation commends your works to another;
   they tell of your mighty acts.
They speak of the glorious splendor of your majesty—
   and I will meditate on your wonderful works.
They tell of the power of your awesome works—
   and I will proclaim your great deeds.
They celebrate your abundant goodness
   and joyfully sing of your righteousness.

The LORD is gracious and compassionate,
   slow to anger and rich in love.

The LORD is good to all;
   he has compassion on all he has made.
All your works praise you, LORD;
   your faithful people extol you.
They tell of the glory of your kingdom
   and speak of your might,
so that all people may know of your mighty acts
   and the glorious splendor of your kingdom.
Your kingdom is an everlasting kingdom,
   and your dominion endures through all generations.

The Lord is trustworthy in all he promises
    and faithful in all he does.
The Lord upholds all who fall
    and lifts up all who are bowed down.
The eyes of all look to you,
    and you give them their food at the proper time.
You open your hand
    and satisfy the desires of every living thing.

The Lord is righteous in all his ways
    and faithful in all he does.
The Lord is near to all who call on him,
    to all who call on him in truth.
He fulfills the desires of those who fear him;
    he hears their cry and saves them.
The Lord watches over all who love him,
    but all the wicked will he destroy.

My mouth will speak in praise of the Lord.
    Let every creature praise his holy name
    for ever and ever.

This psalm is the last of the psalms ascribed to David, and it is the only psalm designated as "A Psalm of Praise" or "The Praise of David"—a *Tehillah*, which is a word derived from the same root as hallelujah. It appears to have been purposefully placed as the last of David's psalms, perhaps to mark emphatically that all his psalms are completed in praise, and in this case of pure praise to God.

As God's ordained king of Israel, David states, "I will exalt you, my God the King." To exalt is to set preeminently on high above all others; it is to hold such a high regard for a person that you endeavor to convince others to believe the same about them. In praising God, David is declaring his devotion to "my God" as one who owns his complete allegiance to "the King," both in the present moment and "for ever and ever." In this life we believe and hope in God, we pray to and praise Him, but in eternity it is our praise that will continue unendingly. Our praise of God will be as unchanging as He is—eternal!

"Every day I will praise you." Our worship should not be conditioned by what any day brings. Whatever our days may hold, whether dark storms or bright sunshine, we will continue to magnify God. Every day is a day to extol and bless His name and person in every sense and way, and not merely for what He has said to us or what He has done for us. The repetition of David's praise reflects his passion to abound in praise forever.

"Great is the LORD and most worthy of praise." The quality of our worship should be in accordance with the worthiness of our God—great praise for a great God. There is no aspect of His greatness that is unworthy of great praise. Our God is magnificent in love, and His kingdom is everlasting. No chorus or group of musicians could be too large or too flawless, no psalm or song too grand for the exaltation of the Lord of hosts.

"His greatness no one can fathom." The Hebrew rendering is, "Of His greatness no investigation," or as the classic Greeks would say, "Not to be traced out." All the minds of all the centuries could never begin to search out the riches of God. He is unsearchable, beyond finding out; and, therefore, the praise that He is worthy of receiving is always above and beyond all that we can offer to Him. When we have studied and searched Him out to the limits of our finiteness, we still find ourselves surrounded with the unknowable wonders of God.

While this is David's own psalm of high praise, we may take it and aim at making our own personal praise as much like it as possible. The best adoration of the unfathomable God begins when we simply close our eyes in reverence before the light of His glory. May we present our own humble praise to the Lord both today and forever!

PSALM 150

Praise the LORD.

Praise God in his sanctuary;
  praise him in his mighty heavens.
Praise him for his acts of power;
  praise him for his surpassing greatness.
Praise him with the sounding of the trumpet,
  praise him with the harp and lyre,
praise him with the timbrel and dancing,
  praise him with the strings and pipe,
praise him with the clash of cymbals,
  praise him with resounding cymbals.

Let everything that has breath praise the LORD.

Praise the LORD.

How could the Book of Psalms end any other way than this? It is as if the great River of Life, with all of its varying moods, its light and shadow, its sorrows and joys, its highs and lows, suddenly becomes a resounding cascade of praise, and this psalm is its grandest waterfall. The psalmist will have every instrument and every person and everything in all of creation pressed into the Hallelujah Choir.

The Book of Psalms begins with "Blessed" and ends with "Praise." As was expressed in Psalm 1, to walk in the ways of God leads to blessedness, and in Psalm 150 our reading culminates in sheer delight and praise. The heart that does God's will in the world may not always experience happiness, but it is always blessed; and when it has patiently allowed God to complete the work He desires, it will ultimately find such joy as to desire all of creation to join it in worship. We may go through many trials, but if we will be faithful to the Most Holy and let Him finish His work in us, hallelujahs will be ours.

"Praise the LORD" is *halleluyah*—a combination of *halal*, or "praise," and *Yah*, the divine name, expressing a command or an exhortation to all things in earth and in heaven. Should they not all declare the glory of Him for whose glory they were created? Jehovah should be the one object of adoration. To give honor and glory to another is shameful and to refuse to offer Him praise is treachery.

All of the various musical instruments give distinct sounds of praise—some quiet; some loud; some having a harmony by themselves; some making harmony with other instruments, but all of them serving to declare God's glory. The very variety of these instruments represents the different men and women who play them and the greatness of our joy at being able to worship God with our entire being.

"Let everything that has breath praise the LORD." There is nothing in the Book of Psalms more majestic or more beautiful than this most momentous finale. By His breath, God created all things, and by our breath, and until our final breath, we will ever adore Him.

LANCE WUBBELS is the vice president of literary development at Koechel Peterson & Associates, a Minneapolis-based design firm, Shiloh Road Publishing, and Bronze Bow Publishing. Before joining Koechel Peterson, he served for eighteen years as managing editor at Bethany House Publishers.

Wubbels has authored several fiction and nonfiction books, including the best-selling gift books with Hallmark, *If Only I Knew, Dance While You Can, I Wish for You,* and *Each Day a New Beginning.* He has published three gift books with Inspired Faith, *Jesus, the Ultimate Gift, A Time for Prayer,* and *To a Child Love Is Spelled T-I-M-E,* which won a 2005 Gold Medallion award from the Evangelical Christian Publishers Association. His novel, *One Small Miracle,* won an Angel Award, and his 365-day devotional, *In His Presence,* also won a Gold Medallion award.

He and his wife make their home in Minnesota.

If you have enjoyed this book
or it has touched your life in some way,
we would love to hear from you.

Please send your comments to:
Hallmark Book Feedback
P.O. Box 419034
Mail Drop 215
Kansas City, MO 64141

Or e-mail us at:
booknotes@hallmark.com